Christian Extremism as a Domestic Terror Threat

A Monograph
by
MAJ Frederick D. Wong
United States Army

School of Advanced Military Studies
United States Army Command and General Staff College
Fort Leavenworth, Kansas

AY 2011

Abstract

CHRISTIAN EXTREMISM AS A DOMESTIC TERROR THREAT by MAJ Frederick D. Wong, United States Army, 48 pages.

Americans readily identify Muslim extremism as a viable threat to America. However, they ignore or remain unaware of Christian extremism in the same context, despite the similarities in ideology that advocate violence against Americans. For example, the motivation behind Eric Rudolph's bombing of the Olympics in Atlanta in 1996 was to "embarrass and punish the U.S. government" for its pro-abortion stance.

This monograph explores what, if any, domestic terror threat Christian extremism poses and follows the Constructivist approach: how ideas define structure, how this structure defines interests, and how actors take action as a result. Initially focusing on the history and core beliefs of the Christian Identity movement and radical fringes of Dominion and Reconstruction theology, this monograph identifies two major underlying themes in Christian extremism. The first is racism through the use of religion as an accelerant to promote violence. The second is religiously motivated terrorism to support what is perceived as God's will and law.

In addition, this monograph analyzes federal law enforcement action against Christian extremism through a series of case studies that took place in Mountainhome, Arkansas, Ruby Ridge, Idaho, and Waco, Texas. The analysis of the catastrophic consequences from Ruby Ridge and Waco with the Oklahoma City bombing follows.

Concluding this monograph are the lessons learned, comparison of federal law enforcement's action in each case study, and analyzing the tactics and leadership involved. Whereas the FBI's tactics and leadership exercised proved highly successful in Arkansas, they were disastrous in Idaho and Texas. Finally, this monograph provides a domestic terror threat assessment with recommended actions in what is not only a law enforcement issue, but a war of ideology between tolerance and understanding versus hate and bigotry. While difficult to implement, the recommended actions contribute to the understanding of Christian extremism and potential threats stemming from it.

Table of Contents

Introduction

They are the media headlines that immediately attract the American public's attention: a truck bomb detonates at a government building, killing 168 and injuring over 600 people,[1] an individual motivated by religious zealotry detonates a bomb at a major sporting event,[2] or a bomb detonates at a church, killing four young girls and injuring 23 people.[3] While sounding similar to what occurs in Iraq or Afghanistan, the described events were not on foreign soil or perpetrated by Islamic terrorist groups. Instead, American citizens committed these acts in the United States in the name of Christianity.

While U.S. policy-makers readily identify Islamic extremism as a dangerous threat to the nation, they fail to view Christian extremism in a similar context despite a common ideology that advocates violence against Americans. Christian extremism is a viable domestic terror threat through two areas. First, Christian extremism preys on an underlying theme of racism by acting as an accelerant and a binding agent for racially-based violence. Second, Christian extremists advocate terrorism on the premise of accomplishing a greater cause, doing God's will.

While there is no universally accepted definition of terrorism, the U.S. Department of State defines terrorism in accordance with Title 22 of the United States Code, Section 2656f (d) as, "…pre-meditated, politically motivated violence against noncombatant targets by subnational groups or clandestine agents, usually intended to influence an audience."[4] The aforementioned

---

[1] Jim Lehrer, "Deadly Explosion," Online News Hour, http://www.pbs.org/newshour/bb/law/mcveigh/news_4-19-95.html (accessed September 16, 2010).

[2] Denise Noe, "Eric Rudolph: Serial Bomber," Turner Broadcasting System Inc., http://www.trutv.com/library/crime/terrorists_spies/terrorists/eric_rudolph/1.html (accessed September 16, 2010).

[3] National Park Service, "Sixteenth Street Baptist Church" U.S. Department of the Interior, http://www.nps.gov/history/nr/travel/civilrights/al11.htm (accessed December 11, 2010).

[4] Edmund J. Hull, "Patterns of Global Terrorism," The Office of Electronic Information, Bureau of Public Affairs, http://www.state.gov/s/ct/rls/crt/2000/2419 htm (accessed September 16, 2010).

events exemplify the components of that definition through the violent acts executed to promote a specific social or political agenda linked to Christian extremism.

Prior to the terrorist attack on 9/11 that killed over 3,000 people, the Oklahoma City bombing perpetrated by Timothy McVeigh on April 19, 1995, was the worst domestic terrorist incident in United States history. Although not motivated by religious ideology, McVeigh was a Christian militia movement sympathizer. His terrorist act was revenge against the U.S. government's 51-day siege at Waco, TX of the Branch Davidians that ended on April 19, 1993, with the deaths of over 80 men, women, and children in their religious compound.[5]

The motivation behind Eric Robert Rudolph's Olympic bombing in Atlanta on July 27, 1996, stemmed from his Christian anti-abortion sentiment. After pleading guilty for crimes he committed in Alabama and Georgia, Rudolph issued an 11-page statement where he declared, "Abortion is murder. And when the regime in Washington legalized, sanctioned and legitimized this practice, they forfeited their legitimacy and moral authority to govern." Rudolph went on to state that his actions were to "embarrass and punish the U.S. government" for its pro-abortion stance.[6]

By contrast, the bomb explosion at the Sixteenth Street Baptist Church that occurred on September 15, 1963, in Alabama, epitomized racial hatred consistent with Christian extremist beliefs. The identified assailant, Ku Klux Klan member Robert Chambliss, would not be convicted of this terrorist act until 1977. Chambliss's motivation stemmed from the racial hatred and white supremacist beliefs that the Ku Klux Klan preached.

---

[5]Jennifer Rosenberg, "Oklahoma City Bombing," The New York Times Company, http://history 1900s.about.com/cs/crimedisaster/p/okcitybombing htm (accessed September 16, 2010).

[6]Emily Lyons, "Rudolph reveals motives," Cable News Network, Turner Broadcasting System Inc., http://articles.cnn.com/2005-04-13/justice/eric rudolph_1_emily-lyons-pipe-bomb-attack-eric-robert-rudolph?_s=PM:LAW (accessed September 16, 2010).

Christian extremism encompasses a wide spectrum of social groups in the United States today. These groups consist of middle and working class Americans who join militias out of fear of an overbearing federal government seizing their Constitutional rights and property, militant anti-abortionists willing to commit acts of violence to save unborn children, white supremacists who believe in Christian Identity theology that advocates racial violence, and ardent anti-Semitic Christians. The methods Christian extremists employ are consistent with those employed by known international terrorist organizations such as al-Qaeda and Hezbollah. These methods consist of explosives, snipers, assassination, death threats, and biological bomb scares and show that terrorism is not solely limited to those who take a militant view of the Islamic faith.

The purpose of this monograph is to contribute to the understanding of Christian extremism and explore the domestic terror threat it poses. It defines Christian extremism in the general terms of extremist religious beliefs and explores the origins of the Christian Identity movement and Dominion and Reconstruction Theories. In addition, it provides case study analysis of domestic terrorists associated with Christian Identity and radical forms of Dominion and Reconstruction theology. Lastly, it examines government intervention against Christian extremism in the United States and its consequences, and proposes recommended actions to be taken against such domestic terror threats in the future. Christian extremism is a domestic terror threat through two major themes: racism through the use of religion as an accelerant to promote violence and religious terrorism to support what is perceived as God's will.

Methodology

The research method for this monograph follows the constructivist/identity approach. Initially, the research explores the origin of the Christian Identity movement and Dominion and Reconstruction Theories, defines each perspective's respective core beliefs, determines how each ideology defines its structure, and then describes how its actors take action within their organizations.

Supporting the constructivist research is case study analysis and comparison of four major incidents involving religious extremism from the Christian Identity movement and federal law enforcement actions taken to counter the domestic terror threat. The analysis reviews the events that occurred and the socio-political aftermath that followed. The first case study involves the U.S. government's action against the Covenant, the Sword, and the Arm of the Lord (CSA), a Christian white supremacist group in Arkansas in 1985. The second involves the FBI's action against white supremacist Randy Weaver in Idaho in 1992. The third focuses on the FBI and Alcohol, Tobacco, and Firearms' (ATF) actions against David Koresh and his religious sect, the Branch Davidians, in Texas in 1993. The fourth analyzes the Oklahoma City bombing in 1995.

A comprehensive analysis centering on anti-abortion violence stemming from radical interpretations of Dominion or Reconstruction ideology follows. Although historically conducted by isolated actors, the assassination and bombing tactics against abortion providers and clinics are consistent with those of well-known international terrorist groups. These actions are terrorist acts meant to promote a religious agenda of militant anti-abortion beliefs and asserting God's will while attempting to intimidate abortion providers.

Finally, the comparison of lessons learned from federal law enforcement operations against Christian extremism follow, analyzing the success, failure, and consequences of the actions and leadership decisions made. An overall domestic terror and regional terror assessment with recommended law enforcement and social actions to counter this domestic terror threat conclude the research. Based on the emergent trends from the socio-political aftermath of federal government intervention and application of lessons learned, the recommendations are by no means easy to implement. However, the proposed suggestions significantly contribute to the understanding of Christian extremism as a domestic terror threat and expand the range of viable options.

Literature Review

What exactly is religious extremism? Is it the evangelist who visits door-to-door and starts the conversation with, "Have you accepted Jesus Christ as your Lord and Savior?" Or is it the Orthodox Jewish family that strictly adheres to religious traditions on dress, diet, and social interaction? Is it exemplified by Westboro Baptist Church members who flash signs that read, "God Hates Fags" and "Thank God for Dead Soldiers" at military funerals?[7]

Religion remains a significantly complex and controversial subject within any social culture. Like any social construct, religion is subject to human interpretation and cultural context. Religious and state institutions that advocate and endorse violence against non-believers of a given denomination on the basis of supporting a divine edict add further complexity to the issues. However, one cannot whitewash the concept of religious extremism with cultural relativism to universally deem extremist actions as justified.[8]

Religious extremism and conflict are not new. Conceivably, as long as religion has existed, the social friction that produces violence stems from differences between scriptural interpretation and practice. Throughout history, religious conflicts proliferated as the various factions accused one another of heresy in some form. As a result, various splinter factions emerged from these conflicts between and among the diverse religions of the world, promoting their more belligerent views through aggression.

Several scholarly works study religious extremism and its relationship with international terrorism. The preponderance of literature focuses on militant Islam and the jihad, meaning "holy war." Surprisingly, few scholars have attempted to define the tenets of religious extremism. Just

---

[7]Anti-Defamation League, "Westboro Baptist Church," Anti-Defamation League, http://www. adl.org/learn/ext_us/WBC/default.asp?LEARN_Cat=Extremism&LEARN_SubCat=Extremism_in_Americ a&xpicked=3&item=WBC (accessed February 2, 2011)

[8]Neil J. Kressel, *Bad Faith: The Danger of Religious Fundamentalism* (Amherst: Prometheus Books, 2007), 50.

as there is no universally accepted definition of terrorism, no universally accepted definition of religious extremism appears to exist due to the controversy centered on religion and issues of cultural context. The result is a lack of general consensus of what defines religious extremism in relevant terms.

In *Bad Faith: The Danger of Religious Extremism*, social psychologist Neil Kressel makes a conscious effort to define religious extremism by considering the impact of religious beliefs, rather than the actual content itself. Acknowledging the diversity of religious faiths and practices, Kressel asserts that while certain religious customs may seem unique, socially archaic, or even dysfunctional when compared to its mainstream practice, those actions would not constitute religious extremism. Furthermore, Kressel discerns that religious extremism is not synonymous with being extremely religious.[9]

Kressel provides a generalized yet functional definition of violent religious extremism, articulating it as "an ideology that calls for committing, promotes, or supports purposefully hurtful, violent, or destructive acts towards those who don't practice their faith or follow its fundamental beliefs." The key aspect of his definition is that the consequences of this form of religious ideology are inherently destructive.[10]

Although a large majority of scholarly work focuses on militant Islam, the concept of jihad, and the psychology of suicide bombers, social scientists have researched Christian fundamentalism as part of exploring the overall context of religious extremism and its conflict against secularism. Mark Juergensmeyer, Director of the Orfalea Center for Global and International Studies and a professor of sociology, stands out from among respected researchers through his extensive research on religious violence. His detailed work consists of personal

---

[9]Kressel, 50.
[10]Ibid, 53-54.

interviews with religious activists around the world, to include individuals convicted of the 1993 World Trade Center bombing, leaders of Hamas, and abortion clinic bombers in the United States.

In *Global Rebellion: Religious Challenges to the Secular State, from Christian Militias to al Qaeda,* Juergensmeyer provides a comprehensive analysis of Christian extremism. Starting initially with Protestantism, Juergensmeyer identifies the emergence of Christian evangelicalism that resulted in a more fundamentalist view of Christianity in the 1960s that later developed into two religious theories: Dominion and Reconstruction. Dominion Theory, synonymous with evangelicals Pat Robertson and Jerry Falwell, calls for Christianity to assert the dominion of God over all creation, including secular politics and society to achieve the fulfillment of messianic expectations.[11] Reconstruction Theory, promoted by anti-abortion/pro-life group Operation Rescue founder Randall Terry, is a more fundamentalist view by identifying the necessity to "reconstruct" Christian society through the Bible as the basis for a nation's law and social order on the premise that Christians are destined to dominate the world.[12] While not overtly advocating violence in a public forum, ardent proponents of those ideas have used violence against abortion providers in their pro-life efforts.[13]

Lane Crothers adds further depth to Dominion and Reconstruction Theories by exploring the Christian concept of millennialism, known in Christian doctrine as the end times where the anti-Christ emerges, followed by the apocalypse. While grim, the event also heralds the return of Christ and his kingdom on earth. However, as Crothers points out in his research of "right-wing Christianity" in a political context, Christians differ as to when this event is to occur. In general,

---

[11]Mark Juergensmeyer, Global Rebellion: Religious Challenges to the Secular State, from Christian Militias to al Qaeda (Los Angeles: University of California Press, 2008), 183.

[12]Ibid, 184.

[13]Ibid, 188.

postmillennialists believe that Christ will return only after Armageddon, a world-wide apocalypse. By contrast, premillennialists tend to believe that Christian values must be imposed on the world. This is prescribed in both Dominion and Reconstruction Theories on the premise that establishing Christian law in practice would ultimately help sinners enter the Kingdom of Heaven.[14]

Juergensmeyer stands out in his exploration of Christian extremist beliefs that stem from the fundamentalism of Dominion and Reconstruction Theories. In addition, Juergensmeyer adds to the consensus of other social scientists and psychologists like Neil J. Kressel and Lane Crothers who describe the Christian Identity movement as the embodiment of Christian extremism. Christian Identity is a fervent ideology of racial and religious bigotry that advocates violence, persecution, and conceivably genocide to promote a divine calling to what its followers perceive as a war for the moral character of America as a righteous nation in the balance. Racist hate-groups ranging from the Ku Klux Klan and White Aryan Resistance, militia groups Posse Comitatus and Covenant, the Sword and the Arm of the Lord, and religious groups World Church of the Creator and Worldwide Church of God, base their beliefs on Christian Identity theology.[15]

It is here, in the research of the Christian Identity movement and the radical fringes of Dominion and Reconstruction theology, that this monograph focuses its analysis of Christian extremism as a domestic terror threat to the United States.

---

[14]Lane Crothers, Rage on the Right: The American Militia Movement from Ruby Ridge to Homeland Security (Lanham: Rowman and Littlefield Publishers, Inc., 2003), 47.

[15]Juergensmeyer, 191.

The Christian Identity Movement

The Christian Identity movement traces its origin to the religious concept of British Israelism. Although initially started by Richard Brothers in England in 1792, John Wilson is regarded as British Israelism's "founding father" by popularizing their beliefs through his book *Lectures on Our Israehtish Origin* in 1840. In *Lectures on Our Israehtish Origin*, Wilson made several bold claims that impacted the racial, social, and religious foundations of Christianity. First, Jesus was an Aryan, not a Semite. Second, migrating Israelite tribes from northern Israel were blue-eyed Aryans who eventually arrived on the British Isles. Third, the "Lost Tribes of the House of Israel" were actually present day Englishmen. Finally, Jews were imposters of God's chosen people and descendants of an illicit affair between Eve and Satan, and were therefore the Devil's spawn.[16]

In the early 20th Century, British Israelism surfaced in America through two major advocates. They were evangelist Gerald L.K. Smith and journalist William J. Cameron. Smith incorporated these ideological concepts in America, preying on existing anti-Semitism to promote his religious and socio-political agenda. Cameron was the publicist for industrialist Henry Ford, reinforcing Ford's own anti-Semitic beliefs while promoting his own through printed media. Both published various periodicals encouraging British Israelism ideas by channeling anti-Semitic sentiment. Smith published *The Cross and the Flag*, a recurring anti-Semitic periodical while Cameron distributed *The International Jew*, Henry Ford's diatribe about an international Jewish conspiracy against social, economic, and government institutions on a global scale.[17]

During the 1940s and 50s, British Israelism became "Americanized" into the Christian Identity movement through Methodist Minister Wesley Swift, a friend of Gerald L.K. Smith. A

---

[16]Juergensmeyer, 188.

[17]Harvey W. Kushner, *Terrorism in America: A Structural Approach to Understanding the Terrorist Threat* (Springfield: Charles C. Thomas Publisher Limited, 1998), 60.

member of the Ku Klux Klan, Wesley Swift popularized what emerged as Christian Identity theology. Also known as Identity, Kingdom Identity, or Christian Israel, Swift modified British Israelism into an American context with a series of declarations. First, the United States is the new Jerusalem, since it was the Anglo-Saxons of England who were the "true" Israelites that settled in North America. Second, the Articles of Confederation, original Constitution, and Bill of Rights are God-given law. Third, for Christ to return to establish his kingdom, God's law on earth must be established through an apocalyptic battle between good and evil. Fourth, Blacks and other people of color are "beasts of the field," a subhuman species. Lastly, Jews are the spawn of Satan.[18]

Emphasizing a divinely ordained racial superiority incorporated with national patriotism and anti-Semitism, Swift's message gathered a loyal following of believers. By the 1960s, retired Army Colonel William Potter Gale promoted Christian Identity ideology to form the Christian Defense League, preaching the same racist message of religious extremism. A former aide to General Douglas MacArthur who coordinated guerrilla resistance in the Philippines during World War II, Gale later formed the radical Christian militia Posse Comitatus in the 1970s. In addition, Gale introduced Richard Girnt Butler to Swift, who in turn converted him to Christian Identity beliefs. Butler later formed the Aryan Nations, a white supremacist group that remains today with a prevalent gang presence and ministry in the California prison system through the Aryan Brotherhood to support its recruitment and promote its ideology.[19]

The Civil Rights Movement of the 1960s and into the 1970s significantly expanded opportunities and legal rights for women and minorities, focusing much of the attention towards African Americans. Other social rights initiatives involved the expansion of abortion rights and

---

[18]Kushner, 60.

[19]Juergensmeyer, 188.

legal protections for homosexuals; this significant social change was a direct threat to the foundation of the Christian Identity movement.

Domestic terrorism stemming from Christian Identity ideology occurred throughout the Civil Rights Movement. In the southern United States, Ku Klux Klan members lynched African Americans and social activist groups as a method of terrorizing the local population without fear of arrest since some local law enforcement officials were members themselves or sympathizers. Despite the violence and aggression, social change in America continued to expand.

Several members of the Christian Identity movement and its associated Christian militias established their own separatist compounds in response to what they perceived as a growing threat to their own religious beliefs and an impending cataclysmic battle. Their ideas of a Jewish conspiracy and a divine calling to preserve racial purity further galvanized their beliefs. These extremist compounds became a combination of commune and paramilitary/ survivalist training camp for an impending apocalyptic end times. For example, in Hayden Lake, Idaho was the Aryan Nations Compound and along the Arkansas-Missouri border was the CSA. Although in different locations, their core Christian Identity beliefs yearned for revolution that would undo America's separation of church and state, provide racial purity, and establish their new society governed by religious law.[20]

The Christian Identity movement and its militias had the organized resources to train, equip, and execute attacks on their primary perceived enemies: Jews, African Americans, and the U.S. government. Their violent acts of aggression and federal government's response to them would have far reaching effects on both sides.

---

[20]Juergensmeyer, 188.

Dominion and Reconstruction Theology

Dominion theology, also known as Dominionism and Dominion Theory, takes its name from Genesis 1:26-31, where God grants human beings "dominion" over all creation. A departure from evangelicalism and a more radical interpretation of Calvinism, Dominionist Christians control at least six television networks and over 2,000 religious radio stations nationwide to promote their message to millions.[21] The most well-known Dominionist Christians are Pat Robertson of the Christian Coalition and Jerry Falwell, founder of the Moral Majority.

Dominionism preaches that Jesus called for Christians to build the kingdom of God in the present, politicizing faith towards the establishment of a Christian state. Socio-political views among Dominionist Christian leaders vary, but the more extreme fundamentalist views consist of the abolition of civil rights laws, labor unions, public schools, denial of citizenship for non-Christians, and the removal of women in the work force to serve in the household. In addition, the federal government would empower church organizations to run social-welfare programs and all schools. The end state would be a godly America where the only legitimate voices are Christian.[22]

Similarly, Reconstruction theology, also known as Reconstructionism and Reconstruction Theory, preaches the reconstruction of America into a Christian state. Based on the belief that Christians are destined to dominate the world, Christian Reconstructionism calls for Biblical law to replace secular legal code. Promoted through social welfare organizations such as the National Right to Life and Operation Blessings that provide support to pregnancy clinics, drug rehabilitation, and other charities, this fundamentalist ideology is immersed in the American mainstream.[23]

---

[21]Chris Hedges, American Fascists: The Christian Right and the War on America, (New York: Free Press, 2006), 10.

[22]Ibid, 14.

[23]Ibid, 12.

The underlying theme of Dominionism and Reconstructionism is the higher calling to do God's will where Biblical law overrules secular law, especially when the secular law is perceived as immoral. It is this belief that motivates militant anti-abortionists to resort to violence to save innocent, unborn children from an immoral law that sentences them to death.

The Covenant, the Sword, and the Arm of the Lord in Mountainhome, Arkansas

James Ellison was a former minister who abandoned mainstream Protestant theology in favor of fundamentalist Christianity before converting to Christian Identity beliefs. Launching the CSA in 1978, Ellison and his followers lived on a 224-acre commune along the shores of Bull Shoals Lake on the Arkansas-Missouri border. As his ideology became more militant, Ellison directed his followers to steal to support the CSA, justifying it through Biblical scripture where the ancient Israelites plundered the Philistine encampment after David slew Goliath. Furthermore, the CSA machine shop provided financial support through illicit manufacturing of machine guns, silencers, and explosives. By the early 1980s, the CSA enjoyed the reputation among Christian extremist and militia circles as being a viable source for illegally converted automatic weapons.[24]

Motivated by a religious ideology that called for violence and equipped with the means to execute it, various CSA members took action to execute their agenda. On August 9, 1983, James Ellison and fellow CSA member Bill Thomas burned the Metropolitan Community Church in Springfield, MS in retaliation for its support of gay rights. In Texarkana, TX, a CSA member killed a pawnshop proprietor on November 11, 1983, after mistakenly identifying him as Jewish. On June 30, 1984, CSA member Richard Wayne Snell assassinated Louis Bryant, a black Arkansas State Trooper, due to his race.[25]

Although committing the act in Arkansas, authorities arrested Snell in Oklahoma following a police pursuit. During this incident, Snell opened fire on police with an assault rifle and a pistol before being wounded then subdued. Once taken into custody, Snell confessed to

---

[24]Daniel Levitas, *The Terrorist Next Door: The Militia Movement and the Radical Right* (New York: Thomas Dunne Books, 2002), 205.

[25]Kushner, 159-161.

killing Bryant. The search of Snell's vehicle by the Oklahoma Bureau of Investigation revealed more startling information. Inside Snell's vehicle was a Mach 10 machine pistol converted to full automatic with a homemade silencer, a .22 semi-automatic pistol, a grenade, CSA literature espousing its hatred, and maps and surveillance documents on a federal judge, an FBI agent, a U.S. Attorney, and ATF agent Bill Buford, who was investigating the CSA for alleged firearms violations. When Oklahoma law enforcement authorities contacted the ATF about their findings, Buford recognized the similarities in this weapon's modification from an arrest in March 1984 involving three CSA members attempting to steal a flatbed trailer. The weapons confiscated consisted of a sawed-off shotgun, a converted Mach 10 machine pistol with homemade silencer, and three .45 semi-automatic pistols.[26]

At Trooper Bryant's funeral on July 5, 1984, then Governor Bill Clinton announced the investigation of extremist groups as a top state priority. Initially, federal and state investigators probed Snell's connection with the CSA. By the winter of 1985, following an extensive combined investigation of the FBI, ATF, and Arkansas State Attorney, authorities assessed the potential of the CSA as a viable domestic terrorist threat. Through informant information, their investigation revealed the conduct of paramilitary training; the construction of grenades, silencers, conversion of semi-automatic weapons to full automatic, and the gathering of information on Jewish businesses as potential CSA targets to attack.[27]

The federal response was to pursue legal action consisted of a warrant to search the CSA compound for illegal weapons. The U.S. Attorney sought prosecution of James Ellison for violating federal statutes on racketeering, the same laws used to arrest leaders of criminal organizations based on criminal activity patterns. To serve the warrant against the heavily armed

---

[26]*The FBI Files*, "Brotherhood of Hate," episode 104, September 22, 2010 (originally aired June 19, 1994).

[27]*The FBI Files*, "Brotherhood of Hate."

and well-trained CSA, the FBI executed a deliberate and methodical operation that serves as a standard for effective tactics and use of force against domestic terror threats.

The operation consisted of three deliberately planned phases. The first phase of the operation consisted of detailed reconnaissance. Augmented by the elite FBI Hostage Rescue Team (HRT), Special Agent Danny Colson headed the special task force. HRT members stealthily executed a slow, methodical night reconnaissance of the CSA compound to assess the structures for possible assault and rescue operations. Additionally, they confirmed the location of the CSA members and conducted a more accurate assessment of the threat faced. There were 65 CSA members consisting of men, women, and children on the 224-acre facility. Based on the information gathered from his reconnaissance, Colson assessed the need for more FBI personnel and not to assault the compound unless absolutely necessary.[28]

The reconnaissance phase and extensive planning for this deliberate operation took ten days. During that time, the FBI successfully deployed over 300 agents into the local community to support Colson's task force without providing an advance warning to the CSA. The FBI accomplished this through the infiltration of agents as fishermen into the local sports fishing camps along the river near the town of Mountainhome, AR. From there, the FBI launched follow-on surveillance using the lake that bordered the CSA compound through fishing boats.

The FBI planned for three possible courses of action against Ellison and the CSA. The first option was to contain, isolate, and negotiate with the CSA. The second was to contain, isolate, and demand the surrender of the CSA. The third was a tactical assault with overwhelming manpower and firepower on the compound, an option that had the highest risk of casualties for both the FBI and CSA. Based on his mission to serve the warrant, the intelligence gathered from

---

[28] *The FBI Files*, "Brotherhood of Hate."

his reconnaissance, and the assessment of the CSA threat and its capabilities, Colson chose the first option.

The second phase of the operation was to isolate the CSA compound. Initiated on the evening of April 18, 1985, Colson deployed FBI snipers and HRT operators under the cover of darkness to establish a perimeter around the CSA compound. By morning, FBI snipers and HRT operators were in concealed positions in a security perimeter to prevent any CSA members from leaving the compound. Colson established his command and control node in the vicinity of the CSA compound gate for the operation. When armed CSA members moved near the perimeter, FBI operators identified themselves and ordered them back inside while successfully remaining concealed; unable to see them, confused CSA members complied and returned inside to notify their leaders of the situation.

The third phase of the operation began with the dialogue between the CSA Deputy, Kerry Noble and James Ellison, with Special Agent Colson, over a period to two days. Since the CSA was a hierarchal military-like organization, FBI negotiator Clint Van Sandt assessed that the CSA leadership would only be interested in speaking to the counterpart tactical commander, not the negotiator. Although reluctant at first and not a trained negotiator, Colson agreed with Van Sandt's assessment and received valuable coaching from him prior to his meetings.

Colson explained the situation to Noble and later Ellison. First, that he was there to serve a federal warrant to search for illegal weapons. Second, that he was aware of how heavily armed the CSA was. Finally, Colson asserted that the CSA compound was surrounded with operators that the CSA couldn't see or fight. Following a two day standoff and extensive negotiations, Ellison explained that not all of the CSA members were willing to surrender and requested Robert Millar, their spiritual advisor, to consult.

Taking what he described in retrospect as a "huge risk and against FBI policy," Colson agreed and had the FBI fly in Millar from Oklahoma to Mountainhome to assist with the negotiation on the third day of the standoff. Although Colson was allowing a confederate into the very organization he was targeting to enter the compound, he assessed that Millar offered the best option given the circumstances for resolving this situation peacefully. Negotiator Van Sandt briefed Millar of the situation, explaining that if Millar successfully brought the standoff to a peaceful end, he would gain the reputation as a peacemaker and leader within the Christian Identity movement by averting the unnecessary loss of life. Millar agreed and after meeting Ellison outside the CSA gate, they entered the compound to continue negotiation. Millar kept Colson periodically informed of the situation and negotiation process, requesting additional time. Colson agreed and Millar remained there overnight.[29]

On April 22, 1985, the fourth day of the standoff, Millar and Ellison emerged from the compound, agreeing to peacefully surrender. Colson warned Ellison of the risk involved if the surrender was a ruse, retaining the security perimeter around the compound. Shortly thereafter, the CSA members emerged unarmed from the buildings in civilian attire, not in their typical military styled fatigues, surrendering peacefully as stated by Ellison. The standoff successfully ended with no shots fired.

The FBI entered its fourth and final phase of the tactical operation, searching the CSA compound. ATF and FBI agents conducted a thorough search with the Deputy CSA leader, uncovering hundreds of automatic weapons, a military grade light anti-tank weapon (LAW), land mines, grenades, plastic explosives, detonators, 30 gallons of cyanide, and an armored car equipped with a machine gun system.

The aftermath put an end to the CSA. James Ellison, the CSA leader, was convicted of federal racketeering charges and sentenced to 20 years in prison. Richard Wayne Snell, already serving a life sentence without the possibility of parole for the murder of Trooper Bryant, was

---

[29] *The FBI Files*, "Brotherhood of Hate."

tried and later convicted of killing the pawn shop proprietor in Texarkana. Sentenced to death, Snell was executed on April 19, 1995, by lethal injection. Deputy CSA leader Kerry Noble served five years in prison for firearms violations and today speaks publicly about the dangers of hate groups. Six other members were convicted and sentenced to prison for CSA-related crimes and the CSA compound is now a collection of abandoned shacks.[30]

Whereas federal law enforcement action in 1985 against the domestic terror threat in Arkansas proved effective, federal intervention in Idaho and Texas during the early 1990s proved disastrous and one of the direct causes to the catastrophic event that followed in Oklahoma in 1995.

---

[30]*The FBI Files*, "Brotherhood of Hate."

Randy Weaver in Ruby Ridge, Idaho

Randy Weaver was a white supremacist who took to the literal interpretation of the Bible. Explicit anti-Semitism, insistence that Christmas was a pagan holiday, and denial of the Holocaust were only a fraction of the Christian Identity-like beliefs Weaver held along with his wife, Vicki.[31]

In September 1983 the Weaver family moved to their newly acquired property in the remote area of Ruby Ridge, Idaho. Weaver's physical isolation from mainstream America matched his ideological isolation from mainstream Christianity. By 1986 Weaver was attending the Aryan Nations World Conference in Naples, Idaho, an outlet to espouse and enhance his religiously driven racist and anti-government beliefs. Weaver met and interacted with other like-minded religious extremists at these events. Among them was an individual named Gus Magisono.

In 1989, Weaver met Magisono again at another Aryan Nations event. During the course of their conversation, the suggestion emerged that Weaver sell sawed-off shotguns to Magisono; they agreed. Weaver later handed Magisono two sawed-off shotguns that he illegally shortened by 5.5 inches on 24 October 1989 for an initial payment of $300 and a promised follow-up payment of $150. Their exchange would be the only illegal weapon sale Weaver made.[32]

Unknown to Weaver, Gus Magisono was an alias for Kenneth Fadeley, a private detective and who periodically worked as a federal informant. Although Weaver committed the act in 1989, federal authorities did not pursue action until 1991. Instead, ATF agents approached Weaver on becoming an informant against other white supremacists in June 1990; Weaver

---

[31]Crothers, 77.

[32]Ibid, 79.

vehemently rejected. The meeting with the ATF reinforced Weaver's already strong, suspicious belief that the government was evil and targeting what he believed to be "real" Christians.

In January 1991, ATF agents arrested Weaver in a sting operation for the illegal weapons charge. Arraigned and released on bond secured through his property the next day, Weaver returned to his mountain cabin at Ruby Ridge and decided not to leave his home again. Ignoring a court summons that mistakenly ordered him to trial on March 20, 1991, when the actual trial date was February 19, 1991, Weaver and his family remained on their property for over a year. Attempts by U.S. Marshals and Weaver family friends to convince Weaver to surrender were unsuccessful.

U.S. Marshals and the ATF decided to intensify their efforts to capture Weaver in what became known as Operation Northern Exposure on March 27, 1992. Similar to the federal law enforcement action against the CSA in 1985, the first phase was surveillance to observe Weaver's routines to create a plan to arrest him with minimal risk to his family and agents. By April 1992, federal agents installed surveillance cameras around the Weaver property, established observation posts, and integrated the FBI's Hostage Rescue Team into the planning. Following an extensive surveillance effort, federal agents identified two clear patterns. One was that whenever the family dog barked, a family member would investigate, and that Weaver and his family members never left their house unarmed.[33]

On August 21, 1992, following their completion of a pre-dawn, close-in surveillance mission on the Weaver home, three U.S. Marshals dressed in camouflage were withdrawing down a dirt road leading away from the home. Randy Weaver, his son Sammy, and family friend Kevin Harris, who was living with them at the time, left the family home carrying rifles. They were following the family dog Striker down the hillside, appearing to be tracking a scent.

_____

[33]Crothers, 81.

Compromised, the three U.S. Marshals took cover in nearby trees, hoping that the dog or family would not detect them. The tactic failed and within minutes the operation escalated into an 11-day standoff with lethal consequences.

Special Agent Arthur Roderick shot the dog while Special Agent William Degan emerged from cover to confront Weaver; accounts conflict if Degan clearly identified himself as a U.S. Marshal or not. Although armed, Randy Weaver immediately ran back up the hill. Harris opened fire, hitting Agent Degan. Degan would die a few minutes later, but not until returning fire with seven shots of his own. Randy Weaver's fourteen year old son, Sammy, was initially cursing at the federal agents for shooting his dog Striker before being called back by his father. When Sammy Weaver turned to run, bullets from Degan's weapon struck and killed him. However, federal law enforcement would remain unaware of his death for the next three days.[34]

Harris retreated to the family cabin and informed them of Sammy Weaver's death. From the federal perspective, what transpired on August 21, 1992 exemplified Weaver's irreconcilable hatred of the government. From Randy Weaver's perspective, his son's death proved his belief of an evil and irresponsible government.

Richard Rogers, Commander of the FBI's Hostage Rescue Team, deployed from FBI Headquarters in Washington, D.C. to Idaho in response to the escalated situation. Assessing the Weavers as a serious and immediate threat, Rogers revised the rules of engagement (ROE) on the use of deadly force. The standard ROE that the FBI followed was to use deadly force only in self-defense or in the defense of innocent personnel. Rogers' revision of the ROE authorized the shooting of any armed adult male on the Weaver compound and encouraged lethal force on sight after the FBI issued a surrender demand.

---

[34]Crothers, 82.

Larry Potts, Rogers' supervisor, tentatively approved the ROE change. On August 22, 1992, FBI snipers arrived, received briefings on the revised ROE, and deployed to their tactical positions. By 6 PM that evening, FBI sniper Lon Horiuchi identified two men and one woman leaving the Weaver cabin moving towards a shed and fired his first shot, wounding Randy Weaver in the arm. Horiuchi fired his second shot as the three individuals fled back to the cabin. The bullet penetrated the door and killed Randy Weaver's wife, Vicki, blowing half of her head from her body.[35] Shrapnel from the bullet severely wounded Harris in the chest and arm. Unbeknownst to the FBI sniper, Vicki Weaver was holding her nine-month old infant daughter at the time.

One hour later, the first FBI attempt at negotiations began. However, from the Weaver family perspective, there was nothing to negotiate, for the government was intent on killing them. The FBI actions that followed validated Weaver's perception. First, the FBI asked for Vicki Weaver to send out the children so that they could be fed using loudspeakers, unaware that she and her son Sammy were already dead. Weaver interpreted the act as malicious taunting. Next, the robot used to deliver a telephone to the cabin front door in an attempt to start a dialogue was still equipped with its 12-gauge shotgun weapon system, further reinforcing Weaver's belief that the government wanted him and his family dead.

The federal roadblock established to prevent external support to the Weavers became a rally point for Weaver sympathizers, white supremacists, skinheads, and any other anti-government group with an agenda to promote. A large contingent of media covering the standoff was also there, interviewing protestors and broadcasting images nationwide of a growing army of federal law enforcement agents and armored vehicles surrounding a family household. To further

---

[35]Levitas, 302.

complicate the situation, law enforcement agents interdicted a group of armed skinheads attempting to breach the perimeter and aid the Weavers.

On August 24, 1992, FBI agents maneuvered to the shed on the Weaver property and found Sammy Weaver's body wrapped in a sheet. After recovering his body and realizing the impact of recent events, FBI negotiation attempts shifted to a more sympathetic tone. However, the standoff would not reach a major turning point until August 26, when white supremacist Bo Gritz arrived at the roadblock and offered to assist in negotiations. A former colonel in the U.S. Army Special Forces, Gritz claimed to have met Weaver in the 1960s. Since FBI negotiations with Weaver devolved to shouting matches, the FBI agreed to let Gritz into the Weaver property.

Gritz negotiated with the Weavers from August 29 to 31. During the dialogue Gritz assessed that the eldest daughter, Sara Weaver, not Randy, was the force holding the family together in the standoff. Gritz was able to convince Randy and Sara Weaver that if Kevin Harris died as a result of the shrapnel wounds that he suffered earlier, Randy would be charged with murder for denying him the opportunity to leave the cabin for medical treatment. In addition, Randy Weaver's own injuries were worsening.

On August 30, 1992, Kevin Harris surrendered outside the cabin and taken for medical treatment. Gritz was also able to persuade the family to have Vicki Weaver's body removed, which they turned over to the FBI that same day. The standoff finally ended on August 31, 1992 when Randy Weaver surrendered for arrest under the negotiated terms of his children being allowed to live with relatives and not be placed in foster care, and that prominent defense attorney Gerry Spence would defend him at his trial.[36]

During the course of the trial, Spence successfully downplayed Weaver's racist beliefs and portrayed him as the victim of an overbearing government abusing its law enforcement

---

[36]Crothers, 87.

authority; an argument easy to promote with the deaths of Sammy and Vicki Weaver. Spence articulated several arguments that attacked how federal authorities conducted their actions. Among them was that if federal agents were not initially planning a violent confrontation with the Weavers, why were federal agents carrying silenced automatic weapons? Another was why did federal agents throw stones at the property, if not to attract the attention of the Weaver's dog, knowing that an armed family member would investigate?[37]

Federal law enforcement's own actions and testimony hindered the government's case against Weaver. First, the government failed to disclose that a member of the Idaho State Police Critical Response Team who extracted the U.S. Marshals from Ruby Ridge reported on August 21, 1992 that federal agents shot first by killing the family dog. Second, FBI sniper Lon Horiuchi claimed that he fired at Randy Weaver and Kevin Harris after someone had fired at a hovering FBI helicopter, a shot that never occurred.

Spence's contentions on the government's conduct continued throughout the trial. In the end, the court found Weaver guilty of only one of the ten crimes charged by the U.S. government, which was the failure to appear in court. In October 1993, Weaver received a prison sentence of 18 months and a $10,000 fine. Having served 14 months in pre-trial confinement, Weaver was free on December 17, 1993, after a supporter paid his fine. Weaver later filed a wrongful death civil suit against the U.S. government that settled in April 1995 for $3.1 million: $1 million for each of Weaver's surviving daughters and $100,000 for Weaver himself.[38]

The aftermath and consequences of Operation Northern Exposure in the context of Christian extremism and domestic terrorism were significant. The events at Ruby Ridge became a rally cry for Christian Identity believers, anti-government conspiracy theorists, and individuals

---

[37]Ibid, 89.
[38]Levitas, 303.

who later joined various militia groups. United by fears of a federal government overstepping its legal authority by targeting lawful citizens with lethal force that became a reality, the Christian Identity movement successfully recruited across a wide spectrum of racist hate groups, middle class Americans, and right-wing political sects. For example, Pete Peters, a Christian Identity leader, sponsored a rally to decry what occurred at Ruby Ridge in Estes Park, Colorado, on October 23, 1992, that members of the Ku Klux Klan, Aryan Nations, Gun Owners of America, and other right-wing political groups attended.[39]

Two key events following Ruby Ridge enhanced anti-government sentiment, conspiracy theories, and Christian extremist beliefs of a morally corrupt government even further. The first was the promotion of Larry Potts to Deputy Director, the second highest position in the FBI, even though an internal FBI investigation and courts deemed the ROE change to be illegal. The second was the guilty plea submitted by FBI Agent Michael Kahoe for obstruction of justice for destroying Ruby Ridge after action reports, specifically those concerning FBI sniper Lon Horiuchi's actions on August 22, 1992.[40]

Despite the glaring tactical errors made and identified by the investigations that followed Ruby Ridge, FBI and ATF leaders retained their preference for lethal force oriented options towards resolving hostile situations over negotiations. This mindset carried over to affect federal law enforcement actions targeting the Branch Davidians in Waco, TX.

---

[39]Kushner, 74.
[40]Crothers, 91.

The Branch Davidians in Waco, Texas

The Branch Davidians were an off-shoot of the Seventh Day Adventist Church. Firm believers of millennialism and an impending apocalyptic end times, the Branch Davidians stockpiled firearms, equipment, and ammunition to survive the aftermath that would follow. Residing in a Christian commune called Mount Carmel in Waco, TX, their leader David Koresh gained the Branch Davidians' utmost loyalty and trust.[41]

While their beliefs did not have the racist overtones or advocate violence consistent with Christian Identity theology, their concepts of a select number of Christians destined to rule are an arguably more radical interpretation of Reconstruction theology. Criminal allegations of Koresh being a cult leader whose group was stockpiling explosives for attacking the government and converting firearms to fully automatic brought the attention of the ATF.[42]

Analogous to law enforcement actions against the CSA in Arkansas and Randy Weaver at Ruby Ridge, federal authorities considered three primary courses of action for this potential crisis situation. The first option was to isolate the Mount Carmel compound and negotiate with the Branch Davidians for Koresh's surrender on illegal firearms charges. The second was to isolate the compound and immediately demand his surrender, and the third was a direct assault with overwhelming force. Although the third option ran the highest risk of casualties and collateral damage for the ATF and Branch Davidians, the ATF planned to execute the assault option. Federal law enforcement authorities maintained an aggressive, assault-first tactical mindset over negotiation in crisis situations, regardless of the lessons derived from the prior failure at Ruby Ridge.

---

[41]Levitas, 303.

[42]Snow, 19-21.

The ATF's preparations were substantial, involving the massing of equipment, personnel, and coordination of hundreds of police and support personnel. ATF agents rehearsed the assault on a replica of the Mount Carmel compound at Fort Hood, TX, for a rapid and dynamic entry operation to arrest David Koresh.[43] Despite extensive planning and preparation, the law enforcement operation executed by the ATF and FBI proved to be an even greater tactical and operational disaster than previous events at Ruby Ridge.

The operation started on February 28, 1993, with a botched ATF raid on the Mount Carmel compound that hinged on the element of surprise, an element the ATF didn't have. Instead of a rapid assault to arrest Koresh, ATF agents faced an armed and well-prepared force opposing them. The ensuing exchange of gunfire between the ATF and Branch Davidians resulted in four dead and twenty wounded ATF agents with several wounded Branch Davidians that included David Koresh. What followed the agreed cease-fire that afternoon was a 51-day siege and failed negotiations involving the FBI Hostage Rescue Team that ended on April 19, 1993, with the fiery death of 76 Branch Davidians, including 17 children, from a final FBI assault on the compound.

The consequences following Waco were profound. Rogers was later removed in June 1993 for his actions and decisions following the Congressional investigation of operations in Waco. The FBI changed its strategies for dealing with religious or ideological extremists, using isolation and "negotiation for as a long as it takes" as the primary tactical option.[44]

In the context of Christian extremism and the domestic terrorist threat, the federal government's actions validated extremist beliefs and conspiracy theories of an evil government targeting Christians and impending end times where "righteous" Christians must take arms and

---

[43]Snow, 20.
[44]Ibid, 110.

fight. Recruitment by Christian Identity activists and related militia groups swelled from various rallies in response to what occurred in Waco and Ruby Ridge. During the standoff at Waco, anti-government protestors and Branch Davidian supporters picketed what they perceived as the federal government abusing its power and authority. At various rallies following Waco, T-shirts read, "Forget the Alamo…remember Waco!"[45] Among the protestors during the Waco siege would be one who took that message to heart and into terrorist action. His name was Timothy McVeigh.

---

[45]Ibid, 110.

The Oklahoma City Bombing

Timothy McVeigh's terrorist attack on the Alfred P. Murrah federal building in Oklahoma City, OK, was revenge for the government's action against the Branch Davidians in Waco, TX. Detonating the bomb on April 19, 1995, exactly two years after the Waco siege ended in the fiery deaths of over 80 men, women, and children in their Mount Carmel compound, McVeigh's terrorist vengeance claimed casualties in the hundreds. Although McVeigh's motivation and method was well-known, further exploration reveals the McVeigh's link to Christian extremism.

McVeigh was a racist who bitterly mistrusted the government, concepts consistent with Christian Identity beliefs that theologically promoted bigotry intermixed with numerous conspiracy theories about Zionists manipulating the federal government. His favorite book was arguably *The Turner Diaries*, a book McVeigh read several times, gave his friends copies, and sold at gun shows. People that knew him described the book as "his Bible".[46]

The book's author, Andrew MacDonald, published *The Turner Diaries* in 1978. In actuality, Andrew MacDonald was a pseudonym for William L. Pierce, a white supremacist who advocated Christian Identity beliefs and was head of the American Nazi Party and neo-Nazi organization known as the National Alliance. His book's storyline consisted of a race war between whites fighting against an evil federal government. The group achieves victory after the mass slaughter of racial minorities and "race traitors" described as other whites that opposed the characters. Among the key events in his story was the destruction of FBI Headquarters in Washington, D.C., with a truck bomb; the exact same method McVeigh employed in Oklahoma City.[47]

---

[46]Snow, 150.

[47]Ibid, 151.

McVeigh and his accomplice Terry Nichols attended various militia meetings, finding an outlet of like-minded individuals venting their conspiracy theories about an overbearing, Zionist-controlled government trying to take their Constitutional rights and plotting against lawful American citizens/Christians. These militia groups adamantly denied McVeigh or Nichols' affiliation with them following the bombing. However, at a minimum, McVeigh most likely felt that he had their moral support from the similarity of beliefs.

In addition to participating among the crowds of protestors and Koresh supporters during the siege at Waco, McVeigh visited the site after Mount Carmel's destruction. McVeigh admittedly wept when Mount Carmel burned with the Branch Davidians inside as his resentment of the government undoubtedly became inflamed into hatred. For the next two years McVeigh conspired with Nichols to retaliate against the federal government; *The Turner Diaries* served as his blueprint for committing the act.[48]

In the context of domestic terrorism, the Oklahoma City bombing revealed two critical aspects of Christian extremism. The first is that the federal government's misuse of force in law enforcement against religious extremists is a rally cry for them, which can spawn domestic terrorist revenge. Whereas the FBI and ATF's patience and effective use of force neutralized the CSA in Mountainhome, their heavy-handed tactics in Ruby Ridge and Waco resulted in several deaths and validated the racist ideologies of Christian extremists of an evil, imperious U.S. government attacking the righteous with an approaching end times, and therefore justified retaliatory violence. The second is that the Oklahoma City bombing demonstrated the magnitude of what Christian extremists are capable of executing. As McVeigh stated in his interview with

---

[48]Levitas, 291.

The Buffalo News, "The truth is, I blew up the Murrah building, and isn't it kind of scary that one man could reap this kind of hell?"[49]

One of the key underlying themes of Christian extremism is racism, as Christian Identity ideology advocates violence and justifies bigotry through a religious context. However, the link between Christian extremism and domestic terrorism is not limited to just racist dogmas, but also in the radical interpretation of the Christian call to save the unborn fetus from being murdered through an abortion.

---

[49]Lou Michel and Dan Herbeck, "American Terrorist: Timothy McVeigh and the Oklahoma City Bombing", *The Buffalo News*, http://gefangener.50megs.com/timothy_mc_veigh/mc_veigh_background. htm (accessed November 27, 2010).

Anti-Abortion Violence

Does a child's life begin at conception or at birth? Is the termination of a healthy fetus murder? Do the unborn have a legal right to life? Should minors be able to get an abortion without parental consent? Should the federal government fund abortions as part of its national health care program?

The questions above reflect the ongoing ethical and legal debate on abortion, a social issue that remains controversial and heavily contested in the United States. Special interest groups contest one another to promote or rescind abortion rights and related health issues such as stem cell research derived from aborted fetuses. Pro-life/anti-abortion groups such as Operation Rescue protest at abortion clinics, opposed by pro-choice groups like the National Organization for Women, stage protests, counter-protests, and rallies for their respective abortion rights agenda.

The religious extremist beliefs associated with anti-abortion violence are linked to Dominion and Reconstruction theology. Both are forms of Christian fundamentalism that believe that Christianity has to be asserted over all creation, including secular politics and society, to fulfill messianic expectations. Taken a step further, an interpretation of Dominion and Reconstruction theology is that religious law overrules secular law.[50] The result is what well-known Christian Reconstructionist and writer of the Dominion theory magazine *Crosswinds* Gary North describes as "vigilante theology."[51] Believing that Christian law overrules the secular law on the issue of abortion rights, these religious extremists commit terrorist acts in the name of God against what they perceive as an immoral law (legalized abortion) for the greater cause of saving the unborn.

---

[50]Kressel, 102.

[51]Juergensmeyer, 187.

The list of domestic terror acts is extensive, designed to harass, intimidate, or eliminate abortion providers, staff, and patients. Many of the tactics employed against abortion clinics and providers are consistent with known international terrorist organizations which employ the targeting and assassination of abortion providers, arson, intimidating threats, and abortion clinic bombings. Since 1992, militant Christian anti-abortionists have resorted to chemical weapons in the form of butyric acid, a colorless liquid with a rancid, vomit-like odor as a weapon against abortion facilities to disrupt services and harass patients and staff.[52] What is simultaneously unique and disturbing is that the individuals committing these terrorist acts are not Islamist jihadists or racial hate-mongers, but Christians driven by the belief that committing these acts are necessary to achieve the greater good of saving the unborn. When arrested, they often willingly confess to committing the act and accept the judicial punishment imposed.

The demographics and tactics of the perpetrators are equally intriguing. Paul Hill was a Presbyterian minister who murdered an abortion provider, Dr. John Britton, in Pensacola, Florida in July 1994; Hill was later tried, convicted, and executed for his crime on September 3, 2003. Another minister, Michael Bray, bombed abortion clinics at night along the east coast of the United States at night in an attempt to deny access to the facility the following day.[53] In March 1997, anti-abortion activist Peter Howard put 13 gas cans and three propane tanks into his truck and drove it through an abortion clinic door in California.[54] On October 23, 1998, James Kopp, a member of the militant Christian anti-abortion group known as the Army of God, murdered

---

[52] National Abortion Federation, "History of Violence – Butyric acid", National Abortion Federation, http://www.prochoice.org/about_abortion/violence/butyric_acid.asp (accessed November 30, 2010).

[53] Kressel, 102.

[54] National Abortion Federation, "History of Violence – Arsons", National Abortion Federation, http://www.prochoice.org/about_abortion/violence/arsons.asp (accessed November 30, 2010).

abortion provider Dr. Barnett Slepian in his home with a sniper bullet.[55] In June 2001, Clayton Waagner mailed hundreds of fake anthrax letters and threats to abortion clinics to disrupt their operations before being caught and arrested. Most recently in Wichita, Kansas, in May 2009, anti-abortion extremist Scott Roeder shot and killed Dr. George Tiller as he attended church with his family.[56]

Overall, there have been hundreds of domestic terror incidents involving assassinations, bombings, bomb threats, and intimidation attempts since the Supreme Court decision Roe vs. Wade legalized abortion in 1973.[57] The recent expansion of abortion rights such as late term abortion and the harvesting of aborted fetuses for medical research have driven a sense of urgency for violent Christian anti-abortionists to save the unborn even more. The fact that Dr. George Tiller was among the few late-term abortion providers in the nation was undoubtedly a significant factor as to why violent anti-abortion activists targeted him. Anti-abortion violence remains a small-scale but persistent domestic terror threat towards abortion providers, their staff, and patients.

Although there is new anti-terror legislation such as the Patriot Act that expand law enforcement surveillance options and increased emphasis on cooperation among the agencies, two prevailing questions remain. First, how do they apply the lessons learned from previous operations to deal with future domestic terror threats? Second, what happens next?

---

[55]Kressel, 102.

[56]Joe Stumpe and Monica Davey, "Abortion Doctor Shot to Death in Kansas Church," The New York Times, http://www.nytimes.com/2009/06/01/us/01tiller.html (accessed November 30, 2010).

[57]National Abortion Federation, "Clinic Violence", National Abortion Federation, http://www.prochoice.org/about_abortion/violence/index.html (accessed November 30, 2010).

Lessons Learned

Federal law enforcement action against the CSA in Arkansas was an extremely well-planned, resourced, and executed operation that diffused a volatile situation and ultimately neutralized a dangerous domestic terror threat. The following areas that will be further explored are inter-agency cooperation, reconnaissance, rules of engagement, escalation of force, and leadership.

The inter-agency cooperation at the federal and state level was essential towards countering the CSA domestic terror threat. The Oklahoma Bureau of Investigation's information sharing with other state and federal law enforcement agencies was critical in the investigation and building a legal case against the CSA. Although the CSA was a domestic terror group that numbered around 65, neutralizing it required a combined effort of U.S. and Arkansas Attorney General's Office, FBI, ATF, and police in Arkansas and Oklahoma.

The importance of timely, relevant, and accurate intelligence gathered from the initial reconnaissance cannot be overstated. Although the FBI had aerial photos and a basic layout of the compound, Colson conducted a stealth physical reconnaissance of the CSA compound at night. As Colson stated in his recollection of the operation, "You cannot command and control a crisis situation unless the Commander has done a recon."[58] Colson and his team's reconnaissance confirmed the locations of buildings and key infrastructures, enabling them to assess the types of building structures in case they needed to assault the facility and gather other critical intelligence necessary for their assessment of the CSA threat in planning. The intelligence gathered proved essential towards Colson's decision to isolate the compound and begin negotiation with the CSA.

The FBI had clear rules of engagement and escalation of force procedures that did not lead to unnecessary violence. With the goal to end the situation peacefully, FBI snipers and HRT

---

[58] *The FBI Files*, "Brotherhood of Hate."

operators employed their rules of engagement effectively, hailing approaching armed CSA members and successfully ordering them to return to the compound. Although capable of employing lethal force, FBI and HRT personnel did not while maintaining perimeter security and not needlessly escalate the already hostile situation.

Lastly, Special Agent Colson's leadership was critical to the overall success of the operation. Colson and his team incorporated the intelligence gathered by other federal and state law enforcement agencies and the reconnaissance into an effective plan they executed. Colson's engagement with CSA leadership in negotiations and the calculated risk of bringing in Robert Millar proved invaluable towards achieving the peaceful surrender of the CSA with no shots fired.

By contrast, Operation Northern Exposure at Ruby Ridge was a tactical disaster that left one U.S. marshal and two civilians dead with significant socio-political consequences related to domestic terrorism. The key points of contention are rules of engagement, escalation of force procedures, and law enforcement leadership.

Based on the mixed response of U.S. Marshals Roderick and Degan when they encountered Kevin Harris with Randy and Sammy Weaver on August 21, there did not appear to be a clear understanding of the ROE and escalation of force procedures for this operation. Degan emerged in the open to identify himself while Roderick opened fire, an act that would predictably generate an armed response from Weaver's group. Federal agents throwing stones towards the Weaver home to possibly provoke their dog and subsequently draw out the Weaver family made their tactical actions questionable.

The decision by Richard Rogers, Commander of FBI Hostage Rescue, to create independent rules of engagement was egregious. At a minimum, the ROE change violated the constitutional rights of U.S. citizens. More importantly, Rogers' decision created a dangerous precedent by making the fear of the U.S. government abusing its authority a reality and resulted in two deaths that could have been averted. In addition, the warrant for Weaver's arrest was for failure to appear in court on allegations of selling two illegally modified firearms; was he really the imminent and dangerous threat the FBI assessed to where lethal force was warranted before the first attempt at negotiation?

The breakdown of ROE, escalation of force procedures, and overall conduct of the operation can be attributed to leadership failures at various levels. For instance, the tactical oversight to remove the weapon system from the robot sent to deliver the phone prevented the start of dialogue between the FBI and Weaver for potential peaceful negotiation. Instead, the FBI's lack of attention to detail reinforced Weaver's belief that the government wanted to kill him and his family, escalating an already dangerous situation. The FBI's lack of situational awareness concerning casualties after two shooting incidents that the federal authorities initiated significantly contributed to why FBI attempts to negotiate failed. By calling for people they already killed through lethal force, the FBI increasingly polarized the situation.

As disastrous as Operation Northern Exposure was, federal law enforcement agency failure in Waco was even more significant and had catastrophic repercussions two years later in Oklahoma City. The critical failures that contributed to the disastrous results in Waco are the lack of tactical surprise, heavy-handed escalation of force procedures and tactics, ineffective psychological operations, obstinate agency parochialism, poor contingency planning, and most significantly, the overarching issue of poor leadership from the tactical level up the chain of command.

Based on its threat assessment of the Branch Davidians and their Mount Carmel compound, the ATF planned a dynamic raid to arrest Koresh while catching his followers unprepared. During its planning, the ATF determined that the element of surprise was essential to successfully facilitate this operation. However, when ATF agents raided the compound, they instead encountered armed Branch Davidians ready to fight what they viewed as a lethal threat to their existence.

The lack of tactical surprise was the immediate result of leaked information. Both the media and later Koresh were aware of when the ATF raid was to occur prior to the assault. On the morning of February 28, 1993, a television news cameraman stopped to ask a mailman for directions to Mount Carmel, leaking that he was covering an impending ATF assault against the Branch Davidians. The mailman was a Branch Davidian, who immediately informed Koresh of the situation. Koresh then spoke to Robert Rodriguez, an undercover ATF agent, telling him that he knew that the raid was coming. Koresh asked Rodriguez to leave the compound and try to stop the assault from occurring. Rodriguez informed his superiors of Koresh's advance knowledge of the operation an hour before the raid was to begin. However, ATF officials still elected to execute this operation without the element of surprise.[59]

The ATF's heavy-handed escalation of force procedures, tactics, and FBI's psychological operations polarized the situation and galvanized the Branch Davidians' will to resist. When the ATF raid started, Koresh opened the door and called out to the agents in an attempt to stop the raid and potentially diffuse the situation. In response, ATF agents opened fire at Koresh, who immediately shut the door as his followers returned fire. The abysmal ATF raid left several agents wounded and dead, starting what became a 51-day siege. In an attempt to degrade the Branch Davidians' resolve, the FBI employed a variety of psychological operations such as spotlights on the compound 24 hours a day and the blaring of aggravating sounds, in particular the sound of animals being slaughtered.[60] The FBI's tactics made what the Branch Davidians believed spiritually a reality; an apocalyptic force of evil was attacking them in the

---

[59]Snow, 21.

[60]Crothers, 108.

form of a morally corrupt government. As the situation worsened, the Branch Davidians' resolve strengthened, countering any viable negotiation effort to de-escalate the violent standoff.

FBI agency parochialism adversely affected its negotiation effort. The FBI Hostage Rescue Team only relied on the advice and assessment of anti-cult activists and criminal psychologists, refusing offers by religious experts and academics specialized in millennialism to assist them. Unlike Randy Weaver, David Koresh actively spoke with FBI negotiators, often discussing his theological beliefs. The FBI categorized Koresh's comments as "Bible babble" and did not attempt to leverage that information towards ending the siege peacefully.[61] Alternatively, the FBI could have used the religious experts' support to interpret Koresh's statements, gather understanding of his perspective, and possibly start a working dialogue towards effective negotiation.

With heavy-handed tactics and efforts that added tension to the already violent situation, escalation towards a lethal conclusion was inevitable. In an attempt to break the siege, the FBI employed chlorobenzalanononitrate, commonly known as CS gas, through converted M2 Bradley Fighting Vehicles into the compound's buildings. Although aware of the flammable risk associated with its use, the FBI and ATF conducted no contingency planning in the event of a fire caused by the CS gas. As a result, there was no firefighting capability nearby. Unprepared, federal law enforcement's attempted arrest of one person ultimately caused the deaths of over 80 others in an inferno that the FBI initiated.

The over-arching theme of federal action in Waco was poor leadership at all levels. FBI Hostage Rescue Team Commander Richard Rogers employed even more heavy-handed tactics at Waco than at Ruby Ridge, escalating violence to a deadly conclusion while failing to arrest David Koresh. Attorney General Janet Reno demonstrated the worst judgment of

---

[61]Crothers, 105.

all at the national level. The overseeing authority for the operation, Reno authorized the use of CS

gas on Mount Carmel, unaware that it was not approved for use in buildings due to its

flammability risk.[62]

---

[62]Crothers, 109.

Threat Assessment

Overall, Christian extremism in terms of direct action against government institutions is a low level threat for federal and state law enforcement officials who face a tremendous challenge. Specifically, the challenge is that Christian extremists who commit terrorist acts are lone actors who fit into mainstream American society, making them extremely difficult to profile and interdict in advance. Whereas the terrorists on 9/11 were part of an international terrorist organization and readily recognizable as foreigners, domestic terrorists such as Richard Snell, Timothy McVeigh, Paul Hill, and Michael Bray worked alone and readily blend in with a common population demographic, white Christian Caucasian males.

Religious and racially motivated hate crimes inspired by Christian Identity beliefs prevail, but remain relatively isolated incidents. Law enforcement's challenge is the interdiction of lone actors committing the terrorist acts. The three-day shooting spree by World Church of the Creator member Benjamin Nathaniel Smith in July 1999 that targeted African, Jewish, and Asian Americans that killed two and wounded nine before committing suicide and the attack on a Jewish community center in Los Angeles, by Aryan Nations supporter Buford O. Furrow Jr. in August 1999 which wounded five and terrorized dozens of children and day care workers are examples of these violent yet isolated actors that are extremely difficult to interdict.[63]

Regionally, Christian extremism as a threat is surprisingly marginal. The recurring issue of illegal immigration and regional border violence has not generated any significant response from the dozens of militia groups that operate in California, New Mexico, Arizona, and Texas. Surprisingly, there were no significant incidents of religiously-motivated reprisals against Muslim-Americans by Christian extremists following the terror attack on September 11, 2001. While various radical theologians and Christian Identity leaders have criticized U.S. policy that

---

[63]Levitas, 326.

led up to 9/11 or applauded the event as a sign of approaching end times, there have been no significant incidents of domestic terror committed against Muslim-Americans or the U.S. government stemming from them.[64]

Nevertheless, a credible threat remains. In the early spring of 2010, law enforcement agents arrested nine members a religious militia group known as the Christian Hutaree on charges of insurrection against the U.S. government. To initiate their war against the government, the Christian Hutaree group allegedly planned to murder law enforcement officers. The Christian Hutaree would then follow-up with separate attacks on the fallen officers' funerals, where a large number of additional law enforcement personnel would likely be attending, to inflict even more casualties in violent, high-profile attacks. As stated on their web-site prior to removal:

Jesus wanted us to be ready to defend ourselves using the sword and stay alive using equipment. The only thing on earth to save the testimony and those who follow it, are the members of the testimony, til the return of Christ in the clouds. We, the Hutaree, are prepared to defend all those who belong to Christ and save those who aren't. We will still spread the word, and fight to keep it, up to the time of the great coming ... The Hutaree will one day see its enemy and meet him on the battlefield if so God wills it. We will reach out to those who are yet blind in the last days of the kingdoms of men and bring them to life in Christ.[65]

However, domestic terrorism in the form of anti-abortion violence remains a highly prevalent threat to security in America. The expansion of abortion rights that allow minors to have abortions without parental consent, late term abortions, harvesting for stem cell research, and possibility of abortions being funded as part of a national health care plan generates

---

[64] Levitas, 335.

[65] Brett Michael Dykes, "Who are the Christian militia 'Hutaree' and why was the FBI targeting them?" Yahoo! Incorporated, http://news.yahoo.com/s/ynews/ynews_ts1361 (accessed September 9, 2010).

numerous socio-political conflicts. All of those issues further galvanize the efforts of anti-abortion activist groups to lobby for pro-life legislation, provide counseling support, conduct peaceful activism, and in some cases, resort to violence. Not surprisingly, abortion clinics now resort to surveillance cameras, private security companies, and local law enforcement for protection while abortion providers and staff wear bulletproof vests. Regardless of the assessment or number of years since the Oklahoma City bombing, the fundamental question remains: how does one stop the next Timothy McVeigh?

Recommendations

Christian extremism has two major underlying themes: racism through the use of religion as justification to promote violence and religious terrorism to support what is perceived as God's will and law. The recommended actions address these complex issues, further expand on them and discuss changes already implemented. While relevant, they are by no means easy to implement. The recommendations are sustainment of negotiation-oriented tactics as the primary option for crisis situations, enforcement of existing anti-militia laws, promotion of racial and religious tolerance, and increased community involvement.

The change in FBI Hostage Rescue Team's tactics from lethal to negotiation-oriented tactics as the primary option must be sustained. The more patient tactical option of "isolate then negotiate" proved successful in dealing with another Christian extremist group, the Freemen of Montana in the spring of 1996. With the assistance of right-wing organizations in the negotiations process, the FBI ended the 81-day standoff peacefully.[66] This not only successfully neutralized a crisis situation and domestic terror threat, but also prevented the incident from becoming a rally cry for Christian extremists and other radical fringe groups towards retaliation against the government.

Although politically difficult to accomplish, the state and federal government must enact and enforce anti-militia and anti-paramilitary training laws. Currently, 17 states prohibit the formation of militias and 17 others prohibit paramilitary training. Among those states, only seven prohibit both.[67]

The militia movement remains a controversial issue. Due to the potential political fallout associated with such legislation proposals, government officials tend to avoid the issue that exists.

---

[66] Crothers, 152.

[67] Snow, 206.

Although small, private armies are illegal and a threat to America and its citizens, given their vehement anti-government and often racist agenda fueled with religious fervor.

Anti-militia laws can be effective against extremist groups when enforced. Morris Dees, co-founder of the Southern Poverty Law Center, used a Texas statute prohibiting private military organization to force the Ku Klux Klan to shut down paramilitary training camps.[68] Yet, state enforcement of these laws remains inconsistent, despite the threat posed.[69]

The most difficult method to combat Christian extremism is the promotion of racial and religious tolerance through education and civic action, all of which requires community involvement. Dozens of watchdog and community action organizations such as the Anti-Defamation League and Southern Poverty Law Center exist nationwide that promote tolerance through education and monitor religious and racial hate groups and associated militias. However, all of these organizations would be inconsequential without the community's support and participation.

Citizen groups can be effective in combating extremist ideology. For instance, in Bellingham, WA, is the Nine Mothers against Hate, a group whose campaign is promotion of racial tolerance. Its campaign involves disseminating messages of racial tolerance, using the symbol of multiracial hands holding one another; the symbol has appeared in homes, bumper stickers, and buttons.[70] In Chicago, the Center for the New Community sponsored a conference and workshop in 1997 to show attendees how to oppose the rhetoric and intimidation tactics of religious hate groups and militias. Starting in 1971, the Southern Poverty Law Center emerged as a nationwide organization opposing racial and religious intolerance through education and

---

[68]Snow, 206.

[69]Ibid, 208.

[70]Ibid, 227.

successful legal action against the United Klans of America and the White Aryan Resistance that forced them to shut down operations.[71]

Combating Christian extremism is not only a law enforcement issue, but a war of ideology between tolerance and understanding versus hate and bigotry. It cannot be solved overnight or ended in a decisive battle, but requires active and sustained community participation. Just as the residents of Weston, MO, with supporters from California and Australia, lined the streets to render honors and family support while preventing the Westboro Baptist Church from promoting its message of religious hate during the funeral procession of Sgt. First Class C.J. Sadell, communities must get involved. [72] As Martin Luther King Jr. once stated, "Human progress is neither automatic nor inevitable... Every step toward the goal of justice requires sacrifice, suffering, and struggle; the tireless exertions and passionate concern of dedicated individuals."[73]

---

[71]Snow, 228.

[72]Magnolia Miller, "Westboro Baptist Church Unable to Protest at Weston, MO Soldier's Funeral", Yahoo! News Network, http://www.associatedcontent.com/article/5985570/westboro_baptist_church_unable_to_protest html (accessed December 1, 2010).

[73]Martin Luther King, Jr. "Martin Luther King, Jr. Quotes", Brainy Quote, http://www.brainy quote. com/quotes/ authors/m/martin_luther_king_jr_2 html (accessed December 1, 2010).

Bibliography

Anti-Defamation League, "Westboro Baptist Church," (Anti-Defamation League, 2011) http://www.adl.org/learn/ext_us/WBC/default.asp?LEARN_Cat=Extremism&LEARN_SubCat=Extremism_in_America&xpicked=3&item=WBC (accessed February 2, 2011)

Associated Press. Yahoo! News. "3 Government Officials: Homegrown terrorists troubling" (The Associated Press, 2010) http://news.yahoo.com/s/ap/20100922/ap_on_go_ca_st_pe/us_senate_terror (accessed September 22, 2010).

Barkun, Michael. *Religion and the Racist Right: The Origins of the Christian Identity Movement.* Chapel Hill: University of North Carolina Press, 1994.

Crothers, Lane. *Rage on the Right: The American Militia Movement from Ruby Ridge to Homeland Security.* Lanham: Rowman and Littlefield Publishers, Inc., 2003.

Dees, Morris. *Gathering Storm: American's Militia Threat.* New York: Harper Collins, 1996.

Dykes, Brett Michael. Yahoo! News. "Who are the Christian militia 'Hutaree' and why was the FBI targeting them?"(Yahoo! Incorporated, 2010) http://news.yahoo.com/s/ynews/ynews_ts1361 (accessed September 9, 2010)

Hedges, Chris. American Fascists: The Christian Right and the War on America. New York: Free Press, 2006.

Hegeman, Roxana. Yahoo! News. "AP source: Grand jury probing anti-abortion murder" (The Associated Press, 2010) http://news.yahoo.com/s/ap/20101009/ap_on_re_us/us_abortion_shooting_grand_jury (accessed October 12, 2010)

Hull, Edmund J. U.S. Department of State. "Patterns of Global Terrorism" (The Office of Electronic Information, Bureau of Public Affairs, 2010) http://www.state.gov/s/ct/rls/crt/2000/2419.htm (accessed September 16, 2010)

Juergensmeyer, Mark. *Global Rebellion: Religious Challenges to the Secular State, from Christian Militias to al Qaeda.* Los Angeles: University of California Press, 2008.

Kressel, Neil J. *Bad Faith: The Danger of Religious Fundamentalism.* Amherst: Prometheus Books, 2007.

Kushner, Harvey W. *Terrorism in America: A Structural Approach to Understanding the Terrorist Threat.* Springfield: Charles C. Thomas Publisher Limited, 1998.

Lehrer, Jim. Online News Hour. "Deadly Explosion" (MacNeil/Lehrer Production, 2010) http://www.pbs.org/newshour/bb/law/mcveigh/news_4-19-95.html (accessed September 16, 2010)

Lee, Robert A. History Guy Media. "Timothy McVeigh" (History Guy Media, 2010) http://www.historyguy.com/biofiles/mcveigh_timothy.html (accessed November 25, 2010)

Levitas, Daniel. *The Terrorist Next Door: The Militia Movement and the Radical Right*. New York: Thomas Dunne Books, 2002.

Linenthal, Edward T. *The Unfinished Bombing: Oklahoma City in American Memory*. New York: Oxford University Press, 2001.

Lyons, Emily. CNN. " Rudolph reveals motives" (Cable News Network, Turner Broadcasting System Inc., 2010) http://articles.cnn.com/2005-04-13/justice/eric.rudolph_1_emily-lyons-pipe-bomb-attack-eric-robert-rudolph?_s=PM:LAW (accessed September 16, 2010)

Mallin, Jay ed. *Terror and Urban Guerrillas: A Study of Tactics and Documents*. Coral Gables: University of Miami Press, 1971.

Michel, Lou and Dan Herbeck. "American Terrorist: Timothy McVeigh and the Oklahoma City Bombing" (The Buffalo News, 2010) http://gefangener.50megs.com/timothy_mc_veigh/mc_veigh_background.htm (accessed November 27, 2010)

Miller, Magnolia. "Westboro Baptist Church Unable to Protest at Weston, MO Soldier's Funeral" (Yahoo! News Network, 2010) http://www.associatedcontent.com/article/5985570/westboro_baptist_church_unable_to_protest.html (accessed December 1, 2010)

National Abortion Federation. "Abortion Violence" (National Abortion Federation, 2010) http://www.prochoice.org/about_abortion/violence/extremists.html (accessed November 27, 2010)

Noe, Denise. truTV Crime Library. "Eric Rudolph: Serial Bomber" (Turner Broadcasting System Inc., 2010) http://www.trutv.com/library/crime/terrorists_spies/terrorists/eric_rudolph/1.html (accessed September 16, 2010)

Rosenberg, Jennifer. About.com. "Oklahoma City Bombing" (The New York Times Company, 2010) http://history1900s.about.com/cs/crimedisaster/p/okcitybombing.htm (accessed September 16, 2010)

Snow, Robert L. *The Militia Threat and Terrorists Among Us*. New York: Plenum Trade, 1999.

Stumpe, Joe and Monica Davey. The New York Times.com "Abortion Doctor Shot to Death in Kansas Church" (The New York Times, 2010) http://www.nytimes.com/2009/06/01/us/01tiller.html (accessed November 30, 2010)

Tetréault, Mary Ann and Robert A. Denemark, eds. *Gods, Guns, and Globalization: Religious Radicalism and International Political Economy*. Boulder: Lynne Rienner Publishers, Inc., 2004.